Lord of Beginnings

Stories of the Elephant-Headed Deity: Ganesh

As told by Radhika Sekar & Illustrated by David Badour

Kaleidoscope Books

Vakils, Feffer & Simons Pvt. Ltd., India

Lord of Beginnings—Stories of the Elephant-Headed Deity: Ganesha
Radhika Sekar
kaleidoscopebooks@rogers.com

Cover Design and Illustrations by David Badour
Ottawa, Canada

Edited by Pollard Editing
Ottawa, Canada
www.pollardediting.com

Price US$ 20.

A Kaleidoscope Book
Published by Vakils, Feffer & Simons Pvt. Ltd.
Mumbai, India

Printed and bound in India

For orders in Canada & USA, contact: kaleidoscopebooks@rogers.com

ISBN 81-87111-68-2

To
Sekar, for his encouragement and support
Nandita, Vikram, Marla, and Adam
Bonnie, Sadie, and Naomi
Also
Maya, Sonia, Diya, Ashton, Megan, Mitchell, Sophie, Toby
And most of all, for Maverick

About These Stories

Hindu mythology is a timeless collection of folklore and legends from the many regions of India that have come down to us through an oral tradition. As a result, they have evolved in many different forms and vary from household to household and region to region.

For example, there are several versions as to how Ganesha received an elephant's head and why his right tusk is broken. In Maharashtra, Ganesha is depicted as having two wives: Siddhi and Buddhi, while in Tamil Nadu he is an inveterate bachelor waiting for the perfect bride.

All Hindu deities have *vahanams*—means of transportation—who serve not only as conveyance but also to assist them in various ways. Shiva's vahanam is the bull, Nandi, Vishnu has the eagle/man, Garuda, the goddess Durga sits astride a lion or tiger, and Ganesha's brother, Murugan, flies a peacock. Ganesha's vahanam is Mushaka the mouse. In these stories, I use the word "assistant" to refer to vahanam, rather than the more awkward phrase "means of transportation."

It must also be remembered that these legends originated in an era when conquests were glorified and heroism was measured on the battlefield. As such, they contain a fair amount of aggression. In the original version of Ganesha's birth, a fierce battle ensues between Parvati's son and Shiva's ganas (forest spirits) in which a host of other gods participate until finally Shiva himself enters the foray and unceremoniously chops off the boy's head with his mighty axe! Similarly, Parvati seems to have no qualms about chopping off the elephant's head for her son.

While such offhand aggression was passively accepted by previous generations, the current one now questions it. Many young mothers admit to me their reluctance to tell children these stories because of the cruelty they contain. "Shiva chops off the little boy's head! How can we teach our children non-violence if the gods themselves behave so aggressively?" they ask.

Fortunately, oral tradition lends itself to modifications and the storyteller is allowed the prerogative to craft the stories in his/her own manner and according to the audience. I have, therefore, rendered these stories in a gentler, less gruesome manner so that the children of this generation may continue to enjoy this integral part of their heritage.

Contents

Beginnings

The snowy peak of Mount Kailash in the Himalayan Mountains is home to the great god Shiva and the goddess Parvati.

Here, while Shiva meditates in an icy cave, lost in his deepest thoughts, Parvati blissfully roams the banks of a mystical lake surrounded by forests of soaring teak trees.

It came to pass one morning as Parvati was thus wandering that she felt the air turning warm.

"Ah," she observed, "the rains are over and the harvest season is near. Soon the granaries will be brimming with grain and there will be feasting and rejoicing."

Golden wheat swayed lusciously in the fields below as the birds nestled their newly hatched babes, and cows, goats, deer, even a tigress in the forest, suckled their infants.

Parvati had no infant of her own and the sight of these forest

mothers made her yearn for a child. Scooping some clay from the warm comforting earth, she skilfully moulded the figure of a little boy. Then, very gently, she blew into his nostrils—*prana*—the breath of life.

Lo and behold! The figure sprang to life and stood before her, alive in every way. A boy—strong, upright, with bright shiny eyes and a melodic laugh.

Parvati clapped her hands in delight and cried, "You will be my son and I will love you dearly!"

The goddess dressed the boy in fine clothes and showed him off to the birds and animals of the forest that came to see him as he played by her side.

The day wore on and by noon it was very humid. The mystical lake shimmered invitingly and Parvati decided to bathe in its cool clear waters.

Turning to her son, she said, "Dear child, please stand guard while I bathe in the lake. And let no one by until I'm done."

"Yes, Mother," responded the boy willingly. "I'll stand guard and see that you are not disturbed."

Picking up a stick, he knit his eyebrows and made his face as fierce as he could. Then he took up his position by the path that led to the lake.

Soon the great god Shiva came by. He too was hot and sweaty in his tiger-skin attire. The icy north wind that was always with him hung limply at his feet.

"I think I'll take a dip," he declared, heading for the lake. But, as he approached, the boy blocked his way.

"Halt!" shouted the boy. "Come no further! My mother is bathing in the lake and no one may approach until she's done."

Shiva was taken aback. The great god was not used to being spoken to in this manner.

"How dare you!" he demanded. "Don't you know that I'm Shiva, Lord of All Creatures? Now, move aside, at once!"

But the boy stood his ground, waving his stick menacingly.

"Who is this cheeky boy?" Shiva wondered irritably. However, not wishing to fight with a little boy, he turned back and sent his army of forest spirits, called ganas, to deal with him instead.

"Remember, he is only a child," Shiva cautioned. "So do not harm him."

But the boy was too skilful for the ganas. Brandishing his stick, he soon sent them scuttling.

"Enough of this foolishness!" thundered Shiva impatiently. "Let me through, you little rascal, or else!"

And the icy north wind blew a gust of frosty air in the boy's face.

The boy, however, remained firm.

"No!" he yelled. "Not until my mother says so!" And, waving his stick once more, he charged the great god.

But Shiva is a yogi and, therefore, strong and agile. With great ease he lifted the boy high off the ground to ward off his blows.

The boy kicked ...

And screamed ...

And yelled, "Let me down! Let me down!"

He struggled fiercely.

Twisting ...

Turning ...

Squirming ...

Until, in the scuffle, ...

In the scuffle, his head fell off and broke into a thousand pieces!

Just then, Parvati came along looking for her child. "Dear me, what is all this noise?" she asked.

Then, seeing the boy laying on the ground, headless, she screamed in anguish.

"My son! My son!" she cried and, turning to Shiva, demanded, "What have you done to my boy?"

Between tears of grief, she explained how she had created him from clay and brought him to life. "And now you have broken off his head!" she sobbed inconsolably, as the animals and birds of the forest tried to comfort her.

Shiva felt awful. He had not meant to harm the boy; in fact, he rather admired his courage.

"I'm so sorry," he said remorsefully. "But the boy wriggled so fiercely … his head fell off and now it is broke in a thousand pieces. There is nothing I can do, unless …"

"Unless?" asked Parvati, looking up, with hope.

"Unless you bring me the head of the first creature you see."

Hastily wiping her tears, Parvati set off, at once, in search of another head.

She went east, then west, and then south. Yet she saw no one. For all the creatures of the world had scampered off into hiding as she approached, fearful that the goddess would ask them for their heads.

Discouraged but determined, Parvati headed north. Here too, all the birds, beasts, and humans hid when they saw her. Tired and despairing, Parvati was about to turn back when she saw an elephant lying by the wayside. He was mortally wounded.

"Dear Mother," he called out. "You seem sad. Pray, what is the matter?"

"My boy's head fell off and broke into a thousand pieces," explained Parvati. "So it cannot be put back. But, if I bring the head of the first creature I see, Shiva will restore him."

"Am I the first creature you have seen?" asked the elephant.

"Yes," whispered Parvati.

The elephant fell silent and thoughtful. Then, after awhile, he raised his head weakly and said, "O great Mother, I am mortally wounded and awaiting death and there-fore have no more use for my head. Grant me a painless release and you may gladly have my head for your son."

Touched by the elephant's generosity, Parvati sat by his side and comforted him until his soul departed. "You will certainly go to a better place," she promised. Then, wrapping his head in ice, she rushed back with it to Mount Kailash.

Shiva fixed it onto the boy's body and—lo and behold! —the boy sprang up again as though nothing had happened. Only now he had the head of an elephant!

But Parvati didn't care. To her, he was still the most beautiful child in the world.

Shiva, the ganas, and all the creatures in the world were also happy. Embracing him fondly, Shiva accepted the boy as his son. Placing a crown on his head, he declared: "Dear one, as you fought off the ganas so bravely you will be called Ganesha and be their Captain. The new head will make you as wise and strong as an elephant and you will be honoured first before all others as the Lord of Beginnings, bringing good luck and great fortune to those who seek your help."

Ganesha trumpeted his joy with his new trunk. And, he did not forget the noble elephant. "Let the elephant be honoured for his noble sacrifice," he said.

"*Tatha stu!* So be it!" chorused Shiva, Parvati, and the ganas.

Thus, Ganesha became the Lord of Beginnings, and, to this day, Hindus everywhere seek his blessings before they start new tasks. Also, in gratitude to the noble elephant, elephants are lovingly cared for in Hindu temples.

Kubera's Pride

Kubera is believed to be the wealthiest person in the world. He owns vast estates in all three worlds—sky, earth, and below. He is so rich that it takes hundreds of bankers thousands of years to count up all his assets!

Shiva and the goddess Parvati received him graciously yet continued to decline his invitation. However, Kubera was so persistent that they finally offered to send someone else in their place.

"We have another engagement," insisted Shiva, politely yet firmly. "But, our son, Ganesha, will gladly attend your feast. Only, make sure you have enough food for he has rather a large appetite."

Kubera laughed haughtily at that. "Don't you know, I am the wealthiest person in the world?" He bragged, "Why, I can feed a hundred boys like Ganesha."

Ganesha arrived at the feast on the appointed day and a turbaned waiter showed him to his seat at the head table.

No sooner had Ganesha settled into his chair than he announced that he was very hungry. "My trip from Mount Kailash has left me famished," he said,

rubbing his belly. "I hope dinner will be soon."

With a snap of his fingers, Kubera summoned his servants.

"You will be served immediately," he declared, adding with a smirk, "—there is plenty of food, so eat heartily, my boy."

The servants brought in an enormous platter of mouth-watering foods from all over the

world. Ganesha's trunk twitched in delight at the aroma. Without delay, he began eating and gobbled down the food in no time at all.

"That was yummy!" he declared, wiping his lips. "But I am still a bit hungry. May I please have some more?"

Servants brought him a second platter, which was more delicious than the first. Ganesha set upon it and soon it was gone. A third, fourth, fifth, even a sixth platter was brought! And

each time, Ganesha would eat every scrap and then smack his lips, declaring, "Delicious! But I'm still hungry."

His belly grew big and round like a pot, yet he was not satisfied. It seemed that the more he ate, the hungrier he became. Soon he'd eaten all the food at the feast.

Kubera, however, was unconcerned. "After all, I am the richest person in the world," he announced and sent for more food from his vast estates in the sky. But Ganesha was still not satisfied.

Kubera then summoned to his vast estates on earth. But Ganesha was still unsatisfied.

Kubera sent out to his vast estates below. Still, Ganesha was hungry.

"But I have no food left!" cried Kubera in alarm. "You have eaten all my food!"

"You told my father that you could feed a hundred boys like me," bellowed Ganesha. "So, give me more food or I will have to eat you!"

And, with that, he began chasing Kubera. Around and around the marquee they went and into the palace. With Ganesha hot at his heels, Kubera fled up, then down, and finally all the way to Mount Kailash.

"Please, please, help me!" he called out to Shiva. "Your son ate all the food at my feast and all the food from my estates in the three worlds. But he is still not satisfied. Now he wants to eat me!"

"Did you not boast that you could feed a hundred boys like him?" responded Shiva coldly.

Kubera hung his head in shame.

The goddess Parvati, however, felt sorry for him. "Give this to Ganesha," she said, holding out a small bowl of rice. "It should satisfy him."

Offering the bowl to Ganesha, Kubera said in a humble voice, "Dear boy, all I have is this bowl of rice. I hope it will be enough to satisfy you."

Ganesha popped the rice into his mouth and let out a mighty burp. "I am so-o-o full," he said, rubbing his belly. "I cannot eat another bite."

Then, yawning sleepily, he curled up on a sofa and was soon fast asleep.

"Kubera, have you learnt your lesson?" Parvati asked sternly.

"Yes, indeed, I have," whispered Kubera meekly. "One should not show off." With a sigh, he tenderly covered Ganesha with a blanket and softly tiptoed away.

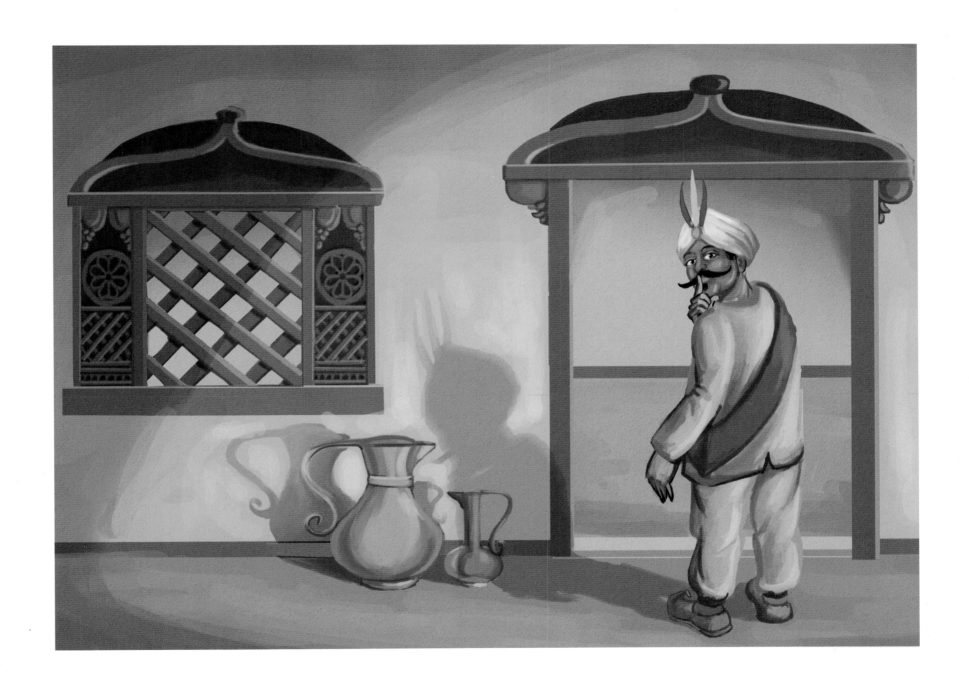

How Mushaka Became Ganesha's Assistant

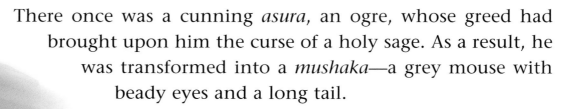

There once was a cunning *asura*, an ogre, whose greed had brought upon him the curse of a holy sage. As a result, he was transformed into a *mushaka*—a grey mouse with beady eyes and a long tail.

This did not, however, stop his greed from growing greater with each passing day. Living underground by day, he would come out at night to steal whatever he could find. But, as he was very intelligent, he soon became an expert at thieving and amassed great wealth.

However, Mushaka was not satisfied, so he decided to appeal to the great god Brahma for more.

Standing on one leg with his arms raised high above his head, he stood for a thousand years in deep meditation.

Impressed by his penance, Brahma appeared to him and said, "You have shown great purpose, my son, so I will grant you a wish. Ask for anything and it will be yours."

"*Anything?*" asked Mushaka, making sure he'd heard correctly.

"Yes, anything," assured the Creator.

Mushaka thought carefully. "My small size allows me to sneak into places where larger creatures cannot go. I am also faster and wilier than most men. But, if only I were stronger, I could carry away more."

Then, bowing low, he addressed Brahma: "O Merciful Creator," he said, "grant me extraordinary strength that I may carry loads that far exceed my size."

"*Tatha stu!* So be it!" pronounced Brahma.

Mushaka now felt tingly all over. His limbs grew hard and muscular and he found that he could now carry loads many times his size.

"I'm strong!" he boasted and became more daring with each passing day. He carried away great bags of grain and bushels and bushels of fruit. He became so bold that he chased away cats, pillaged crops in the field, terrorized housewives in their kitchens, and frightened babies in their cradles. Wherever he went, he knocked things down and created a commotion as he sped away.

All the other mice were impressed by Mushaka's strength and elected him their Chief. Organizing them into an army, Mushaka led them on raids. They pillaged all the granaries in the area.

Mushaka's infamy spread far and wide. Villagers everywhere began to dread him. "He must be caught!" they shrieked, and set traps. But he was too fast and clever; and besides, no trap was strong enough to hold him.

That year the harvest was bountiful and the King declared a special thanksgiving celebra-

tion. Sacks of rice, lentils, sugar cane, and coconuts were brought to the royal kitchen in preparation for the feast. There were bushels of fruits and vegetables, honey, and other edible treats.

When Mushaka heard about the feast he became very excited and called a meeting of his followers.

"The King is holding a great feast," he announced, his eyes sparkling with greed. "There will be plenty for us to raid. So, follow me to the royal kitchen!"

With a great cheer, the mice fell into line and followed Mushaka, shouting: "To the royal kitchen!"

Being so small, they easily snuck in through tiny cracks in the walls and began carrying away sacks of grain—through the kitchen door, for the sacks would not fit back through the tiny cracks.

When the Royal Cook saw the dwindling supplies, he alerted the guards, who rushed in to capture the pesky mice. But, the little mice scattered in a hundred directions, leaving the guards hopping mad.

The King was very distressed when he heard about it. "This is all Mushaka's doing," he grumbled. "He must be stopped!"

He sent his army to capture Mushaka and they caught him and tied him up. But, within seconds, the little mouse gnawed through their ropes and ran off, laughing.

Finally, the King appealed to the elephant-headed Ganesha for help.

"O Remover of Obstacles!" he pleaded. "Mushaka is a nuisance. If he keeps raiding our supplies, we will have nothing left for the feast. Please, help us."

Gathering his weapons, Ganesha went in search of the mouse. But when Mushaka saw Ganesha rambling towards him, with his great belly and elephant's head rolling from side to side, he laughed out loud. "Look how clumsy he is!" he roared. "Surely, he does not expect to catch me."

Coming close to Ganesha, he thumbed his nose at him and ran off. But, knowing that Mushaka's overconfidence would be his downfall, Ganesha waited patiently.

Mushaka came closer…

Closer …

Still closer …

Until he was very, very close …

Making a face at the god, he was about to run off when Ganesha pounced on him with lightening speed.

Caught by surprise, Mushaka tried to dash away, but Ganesha stre-e-e-tched his trunk as far as it would go and grabbed hold of Mushaka's long tail.

At last! Mushaka was caught!

"Now, what shall I do with you?" mused Ganesha, dangling Mushaka by his tail.

"Spare me, please, O Elephant-Headed One!" pleaded Mushaka. "You who are known for your mercy. Set me free and I will serve you faithfully."

"But you are cunning and greedy," replied Ganesha.

"I promise to mend my ways," entreated Mushaka.

"H'm," said Ganesha thoughtfully, "you are fast and clever and have enormous strength. These qualities could be put to good use. And, I do need an assistant. Besides, if you are constantly by my side, I can keep an eye on you. All right, Mushaka, you may serve me. Together, we will travel the four corners of the world, helping those in need."

And that's how the small grey mouse with the long tail and beady eyes became Ganesha's assistant and put his intelligence to good use.

How Ganesha's Tusk Got Broken

The Ganesha festival falls after the rainy season on the fourth day of the Indian month of *Bhadrapada* (from September 15th to October 15th). On this day, Hindus everywhere give thanks for the harvest. They prepare special feasts, including Ganesha's favourite dessert: a sweet dumpling called *modaka*, which is made of rice flour stuffed with lentil, sugar, and coconut.

During the festival, Ganesha and Mushaka visit the homes of everyone who celebrates the festival, bringing good luck for the next year.

One year, the harvest was particularly good and the granaries were overflowing. People were very happy and had prepared all kinds of tasty food and delicacies, especially great quantities of modakas.

Ganesha's trunk twitched in delight as it picked up the sweet aromas.

"Aha!" he cried in delight. "Modakas! My favourite sweet." And, pausing at each house, he made for the sweets that were set out for him and ate until he finished everything on the platter. Then, burping contentedly, he moved on to the next house.

This went on until the sun went down and the moon rose high. There was only one village left on Ganesha's list, so, loosening his belt, Ganesha climbed onto Mushaka's back and ordered him to carry him there.

Now, the great god Brahma had granted Mushaka enormous strength and normally the little mouse could easily carry Ganesha. But, this season, the Elephant-Headed One had eaten so much and had gained so much weight that his little assistant collapsed under his load.

"O master, forgive me!" cried Mushaka. "You are too heavy for me. Wouldn't you like to walk instead?"

"Nonsense!" replied Ganesha, climbing back onto Mushaka. "I'm the same as always. Now hurry. People in the next village are waiting and I cannot disappoint them."

But poor Mushaka collapsed again, this time sending his master flying to the ground.

Just then, a loud chuckle was heard from the sky. Chandra, the moon, was watching the scene with great amusement.

"Ha, ha, ha!" he laughed in his silvery voice. "What a funny sight. An elephant riding a mouse!"

His dignity hurt, Ganesha picked himself up and yelled crossly, "Stop it! It's not nice to laugh at me!"

But Chandra only laughed harder. "Hee, hee, hee!"

Losing his temper, Ganesha broke off one of his tusks and threw it angrily at the moon. There was a loud crack as his tusk hit Chandra.

All became dark, for the gleaming moon that had brightened the night sky had smashed into pieces! Only a tiny sliver that hardly cast any light remained in the sky.

The stars trembled in confusion. Tides kept rising and oceans swelled. Surya, the sun, fell into a quandary and forgot to rise in the morning. The whole world was thrown into panic.

"See what your teasing has done, Chandra?" scolded the great god Shiva. "And, Ganesha, by losing your temper you not only broke your tusk, but destroyed the balance of night and day. Now, set it right, at once!"

Full of remorse, Ganesha set out to make amends.

"O Chandra," he said, holding out a friendly hand. "You should not have laughed at me, and I should not have lost my temper. For this, we have both paid dearly. Now, listen carefully to what I am about to say. For fifteen days, you shall grow larger until you are once more the glowing disc that you once were, lighting up the night sky. Then, to remind you not to tease others, you will grow smaller for the next fifteen days until you disappear. This will be your journey through the months, over and over again, for all time."

Then, turning to little Mushaka, Ganesha reluctantly admitted that perhaps he was a bit too heavy. "I will walk to the next village," he said. "The exercise will do me good. Hop onto my shoulder and I will give you a ride."

Mushaka climbed onto Ganesha's shoulder and the two continued to the next village.

And those on earth, who celebrate the festival of Ganesha on the fourth night after the new moon in the Hindu month of Bhadrapada, take care not to look at Chandra. For he must be ignored for laughing at Ganesha. As for the Elephant-Headed One, his broken tusk is a constant reminder of the time he lost his temper.

Ganesha and his brother, Murugan, are opposites in every way. While Ganesha is large and bulky, Murugan is slim and nimble. Whereas Ganesha rides a little mouse, Murugan speeds through the sky on a splendid peacock of many colours.

The brothers love each other very much, but, like all siblings, they sometimes quarrel.

"I have the strength of six men," bragged Murugan.

"So!" shouted back Ganesha. "With my trunk, I can uproot great trees."

"People say I'm handsome," rejoined Murugan.

"But I am brave, so brave that Father made me Captain of the Ganas," retorted Ganesha.

And so they bickered and argued. Each trying to outdo the other until their father, the great god Shiva, could bear it no longer.

"You are disturbing the peace of Mount Kailash," he grumbled. "Now settle your differences quickly and let us have some quiet."

However, the brothers would not stop quarrelling. So, in the end, Shiva suggested a contest to settle their dispute. "The winner will be rewarded with a juicy golden mango."

Murugan agreed at once. "Yes!" he cried eagerly. "I know! We'll race around the world. Whoever returns first will be the winner."

Ganesha was not too sure about this. Although they were equally strong and brave, Murugan's peacock was as swift as the wind. Ganesha's Mushaka was no match for him. But, not wishing to appear weak, he agreed reluctantly.

They took their positions and, when Shiva gave the signal, Murugan took off with lightening speed on his splendid peacock.

Mushaka, on the other hand, staggering under the weight of his master, wobbled a few feet and collapsed in a heap. No amount of coaxing could revive him.

"What am I to do?" wailed Ganesha. "Mushaka has collapsed and I have nothing to ride. How can I race around the world? I will have to admit defeat."

Crestfallen, he sat down on the wayside with his head in his hands.

Now, Mushaka was very cunning and he thought of something, which he whispered in Ganesha's ear. The Elephant-Headed One jumped up, excitedly crying, "Yes, I think it can work!"

Calling his parents together, Ganesha asked them to stand side by side. Then he went around them three times.

"Dear Father," he said, bowing respectfully, "declare me the winner, for I have just been around the world not once, but three times."

"How could you have done that so soon?" asked a puzzled Shiva. "I did not see you leave."

"Father," explained Ganesha solemnly, "the sages say that you are Spirit and Mother Parvati is Form and together you make up the entire world. Therefore, going around you both is indeed circling the world."

Shiva and Parvati were impressed by Ganesha's cleverness. Handing him the mango, Shiva said, "What you lack in speed my son, you make up for in wit.
I therefore declare you the winner."

Shortly thereafter, Murugan flew in. Imagine his outrage when he found that Ganesha had outwitted him.

"Not fair!" he cried out, stamping his feet.

"Let us share the mango," suggested Ganesha kindly.

And the two brothers were friends again and there was peace once more on Mount Kailash.

A Perfect Bride for Ganesha

When Ganesha grew to manhood, his parents—the great god, Shiva, and the goddess, Parvati, —decided that it was time for him to marry.

"Dear son," they said, "let us find you a beautiful, warm-hearted bride who will love you and be your life's companion."

Now, the Lord of Beginnings did indeed wish to marry, for he was tired of his bachelor life. Nevertheless, like many young men, he was anxious for a bride who was perfect in every way.

"Dear parents," he replied, "I do, indeed, wish to marry. But I would like a bride both beautiful and warm-hearted, *and* wise."

Shiva and Parvati were sympathetic to their son's concerns and assured him that they would choose very carefully.

Hearing that the mighty ocean had a daughter, they approached him, saying, "O mighty Sagar. We are in search of a bride who will love our son dearly and forever be his life's com-

panion. We hear that you have a daughter who is beautiful, warm-hearted, *and* wise."

"Indeed, I do," replied Sagar, proudly presenting his daughter to the young groom-to-be. "And, she is as lively as the waves."

But the Elephant-Headed One shook his great head, saying, "Nay, she is too high-spirited. I want my bride to be calm."

Shiva and Parvati then approached Vindhya—the mighty mountain in central India.

"O mighty Vindhya," they said, "we are looking for a bride who will love our son dearly and forever be his life's companion. We hear that you have a daughter who is beautiful, warm-hearted, wise, *and* calm."

"Indeed, I do," replied Vindhya, proudly presenting his daughter to the young man. "And, she is as steady as a rock."

But the Pot-Bellied One shook his mighty head again and said, "Nay, she is too rigid. I would like my bride to be supple."

His parents then approached the King of Heaven. "O great Indra," they said, "we are searching for a bride who will love our son dearly and be forever his life's companion. We hear that you have a beautiful daughter who is warm-hearted, wise, calm, *and* supple."

"Indeed, I do," replied Indra, proudly presenting his daughter to the young bachelor. "And, she dances like the wind."

But the One with the Broken Tusk shook his enormous head and said, "Nay, but does she sing? I would like my bride to be as melodic as a songbird."

By now, Shiva and Parvati were losing patience with their son. They decided to try one more time.

Approaching the great god Brahma, they said, "O Brahma, we are in search of a bride who will love our son dearly and be forever his life's companion. We hear that you have a beautiful daughter who is warm-hearted, wise, calm, supple, dances like the wind, *and* is as melodic as a songbird."

"Indeed, I do," replied Brahma, proudly presenting his daughter. "And, she is also modest."

But, again, Ganesha shook his elephant head and said, "Nay, she is too timid."

"I give up!" shouted Shiva, throwing his hands in the air.

The goddess Parvati was more patient. "Dear son," she said, putting her arm about Ganesha's shoulders, "tell me what you are looking for and I will try to find such a bride."

Shyly, Ganesha replied, "I wish my bride to have all of the qualities mentioned before and then some. I wish her to be perfect in every way."

"Ah, my dear boy," replied Parvati, shaking her head. "If it's perfection you seek then you will have to wait an eternity. For in truth, no one in this world is perfect."

"Then I shall not marry," pouted Ganesha, letting his trunk hang limp.

Seeing his disappointment, Parvati suggested that he go and wait by the temple door.

"Who knows," she said, "perhaps you will be fortunate and a maiden of the perfection you seek will eventually come by."

Brightened by her words, Ganesha called his trusted Mushaka and the two went to wait by the temple door.

And there they sit to this day, waiting and waiting for the perfect bride.

About the Author

Born in India, Radhika has lived in Canada since 1974. She holds a PhD in Religious Studies and taught courses on Hinduism at Carleton University and University of Ottawa . She has now turned her interests to creative writing.

Radhika points out that the Hindu religion is not structured in the same manner as Christianity, Judaism, or Islam, where children are formally taught their scriptures. Hindu children learn through practice, observation, and storytelling. This is easy in India where the predominant culture is Hindu. She heard many of these stories as a child from her parents, grandparents, aunts, uncles, *ayah*, *chowkidar*, (watchman) —in fact, any adult who had time to spare. But in minority situations like Canada, a conscious effort has to be made to teach religion to the young and it was while bringing up her two children in such a situation that she realized the need for books on Hindu legends and themes. She hopes that this book and others in the Kaleidoscope Books series will fill that void and encourage children of all backgrounds and ages to learn more about Hindu culture.

Forthcoming titles in the series are: *Legends of Divali, Krishna, Stories from the Vedas* and, *The Book of Asuras*.

Radhika now resides in Ottawa with her husband.

About the Illustrator

A graduate of Sheridan College in 1993, David Badour has been working as an illustrator and graphic designer for ten years. During this time he has completed artwork published in books, animated television series, magazines, and children's interactive CD-ROMs.

As an enthusiast of comparitive religion, David is honoured to help perpetuate and transmit the rich cultural and religious traditions found in the stories of Ganesha. He now resides in Ottawa with his wife and two children.